Candle-light

Story by Beverley Randell
Illustrations by Nathalie Ortega

"Ben, it's dinner time,"
said Mum, one wet night.

"I'm coming," said Ben.

Then, all the lights went out.

"Help! I can't see you," said Ben.

"I'm here by the window,"
said Mum.

Ben went to the window
and he looked up the road
at the houses.
No one had a light on.
No one.

"Where did I put the candles?"
said Mum.

"They are up there," said Ben.

"Good boy," said Mum.

They had dinner
in the yellow candle-light.

"I like candles," said Mum.

"Me too," said Ben.
"This is good fun."

At bedtime, Ben and Mum went
into the bathroom with a candle.
Ben sang a little song.

This is the way I clean my teeth,
I clean my teeth, I clean my teeth.
This is the way I clean my teeth,
I like my yellow candle.

They went into Ben's bedroom
with the candle …
but before he got into bed,
the lights came on!

"Oh, Mum!" said Ben.
"The lights have come on!
I **liked** my candle.
I don't want to turn it off."

Mum smiled,

and she put the lights out.

"You can have a candle,"

she said, and **she** sang a song.

Here comes a candle

to light you to bed,

and here comes a ***story***

for Ben and for Ted.

And then, after the story,
Mum turned the candle off.